Tenderness
Tim Dooley

Smith/Doorstop Books

Published 2004 by
Smith/Doorstop Books
The Poetry Business
The Studio
Byram Arcade
Westgate
Huddersfield HD1 1ND

Copyright © Tim Dooley 2004
All Rights Reserved

ISBN 1-902382-64-1
Typeset at The Poetry Business
Printed by Peepal Tree, Leeds

The Poetry Business gratefully acknowledges the help of
Kirklees Metropolitan Council and Arts Council England.

Acknowledgements
Some of these poems have appeared previously in the
following publications: *Cracked Lookingglass, Exeter
Poetry Prize Anthology 1997, The North, Numbers, The
Observer, Poetry London Newsletter, Poetry Oxford, Sheffield
Thursday, Smiths Knoll, Southern Review (USA), Swansea
Review, Times Literary Supplement*.

'Pornography' won first prize in the 1995 Sheffield Thursday
Poetry Competition. 'Tenderness' was a winning poem in
The Blue Nose Poet of the Year Competition 2001

CONTENTS

5	Night Shift
6	Y Habra Trabàjo Para Todos
7	Resistance
8	Tenderness
10	Narcissus
12	The Apiarists
14	September
15	Seeing Shelley Plain
16	Contre-jour
17	Fading Chameleons
18	Mrs. Wu
20	Tidying Up
22	Pornography
23	Echoes
24	Customs of the Province
25	Yes it is
26	After Neruda
27	A Salesman in the Lakes
28	Tact
30	Cellular
31	Chez Haynes
32	The Length of Spring

for my mother

NIGHT SHIFT

We're like night-watchmen,
our eyes more salmon-red
at each hour's end, but not
from crying or a dream's
disturbance – we're pastors
naming every item left at risk,
all to be lost should sleep
disturb our husbandry.

after 'Le Travail du Poète' by Phillipe Jaccottet

Y HABRA TRABÀJO PARA TODOS

Canary, scarlet, oatmeal, azure, green.
I like the green best I think – the colour
of a young leaf or just ripe capsicum –
used here for half a face, or the profile
of a face, all but the pouch under one eye
that masquerades as a full-bellied dove.

A woman's bare arm – impossibly long –
unfolding sheaves of wheat, posters, what might be
rolls of cloth; more faces split by stalks; a clenched
fist clutching a flashlight or pick-handle,
holding up, in the patchy blue,
the bright lonely star of his country's flag.

Among the waxy cookery smears and jagged
blu-tack scars on our uneven kitchen wall,
the caption's bold lettering survives
with this ambiguous promise; for sixteen years
it's earned its place – this message from Allende's
republic – AND THERE WILL BE WORK FOR ALL.

RESISTANCE

Days after the storm, this unsought fog
holds fireworks' aftersmoke, while streetlights blink
a wasteful orange forgetful of clocks.

Yellow and pale and brown, our hectic walk
to school fills with fragmented leaves,
faces passing, familiar multitudes.

And Shelley was wrong too about the way
the dying leaves hold to the damaged branch
against the force of theory or wind.

Leaves cling like all of us, to purposes
imagined once – the wound forgotten spring
still uncoiling in our steps

TENDERNESS

Is it six weeks since he started to scan
the green perimeters of towns like these,
skirt small-scale neighbourhoods for playing fields
whose mists give way to the thin metal legs
of institutional tables? Today he walks
along a gaping line of opened hatches –
Volvo Estates or sun-roofed Sierras –
noting cardboard-housed crockery, batches
of film magazines, one ironing board
burn-stained, little-worn suits and dresses.
He's looking, if asked, for electrical goods
but has in mind a certain twin-tone box,
coated in thin plastic, latched like luggage,
he'll recognise even from this distance.

The cream loudspeaker grille might be badly
yellowed, or chipped near one of its curved
corners, but he'll pull out a sheaf of notes.
He'll take the Dansette home and then search out
(among loft debris, dusty mementoes
of his children's childhood) the paper bags
that store – some scratched and most in mismatched
sleeves – his old black vinyl discs. Sifting
Parlophone pound signs, ears labelled
eff eff double r, he'll select eight singles
to stack on the still shiny central spindle
and shift the arm across.

              Then he'll notice
he's chosen Soul records mostly: dance
numbers where the word *man* repeats itself
or gets stretched across three bars by Percy Sledge.

None of them stick or jump and the last brings
Otis Redding's voice, soaring pure against
the tinny unimpressive backing sound,
imploring him to *try a little*. And that word.

NARCISSUS

Neither sliding request-slips
across the central desk,
nor making tall, curved shelves
his point of landfall
as he pilots himself back
to a numbered, lettered space
beyond the stretching spokes
of others' loaded tables

– returning to his text
is when the word *reflection*
suggests itself; and tapping
some quiet rhythm on his teeth
with a pencil, it becomes
imposed on his regard.

The face that swims towards him –
breaking a surface of language
a hundred and forty years
seem scarcely to have troubled –
is no other than his own;
where else to find repeated
the shameful hesitations,
the penetrating stare?

Was the great half-globed room
– silent mill of learning –
itself set up for this?
Dusty hand-held mirrors
peered at for a second glimpse
of our own returned desire?

A bell rings. Readers shuffle into line.
A man in jeans and gold-rimmed specs
hands back a lightly annotated Plath.
The elegant, tall woman ahead
keeps her Napoleon on hold.

Books crash on trolleys,
disappear to stacks.
The legendary echo
is what disturbs him most.

THE APIARISTS

Beneath the gauze, his lips
are licked tight
on a message sealed long ago,
folded over and turned down
like the rejection of a smile.

His short chin is propped up
by fleshy rings of neck;
everything else in his face
is on the point of collapse
– except the gaze:

intent on the Fancy,
the proceedings of the convention.
He prepares a stinging comment
on the organization's honour,
its insufficient rules.

His co-delegate
wears a striped hat
from which black ringlets fall.
He is here for the buzz
of debate, the company

of workers in his field
and will not complain
if the lecture drones on half an hour
past schedule. He is young.
It's his first time here.

He's growing a beard.
Who is there to tell him
how his passion can harden
to a dark and sticky
concentration of cells ?

SEPTEMBER

He's begun reading biographies
and noticing how the cramped
early pages, the three
contrasting accounts
of how the lovers met

give way to vaguenesses,
gaps filled with speculation,
years when the subject might
have visited Tuscany
or acted in an undistinguished role

of which records later vanished.
So, after Sunday lunch,
it seems natural to walk
through the park unnoticed,
or watch others wander past

without acknowledgement,
kicking a crab apple perhaps,
or prising a conker open,
exposing its shiny
coffin-shaded fruit.

SEEING SHELLEY PLAIN

The tall figure with feathering
white hair, crossing the foyer
of the Queen Elizabeth Hall
as if on castors, one arm aloft
holding the largest glass of vodka
in the world, as if this were
the Statue of Liberty's lamp
(and he Paul Revere)
was Robert Lowell.

And when the Poetry Society flunky
added to his censure of flashes
that smoking was not permitted,
Auden's dried apricot face snarled
that he liked cigarettes,
but cameras interfered with his reading.
And what a reading. Parts of the Eddas.
'In Praise of Limestone'. Favourites back to the thirties.

You could get Bunting then.
'Briggflatts' almost too often,
but 'Chomei at Toyama' unforgettably
and 'a piece W. B. Yeats did me the honour
of learning by heart'.
Somehow, in the downstairs bar,
we got to talking about how Homer
would have fared on the wireless.

I never saw Stevie Smith (though
my brother did) and I later met people
who'd met David Jones. At college
I vaguely knew a man called Trueblood
who in Venice, on his way from Santa Barbara,
saw almost the last of Ezra Pound,
silent between two aged women.

CONTRE-JOUR

> *(portraits of Ezra Pound)*

that mastery of ink and brush
                the chisel's grave hierarchy
                              accepted
but Avedon's photograph
        6.30.58
                          Rutherford New Jersey
cut citrus sun-dried
              a thin shirt draped
                        on the coarse cloth skin
they saved for him
              sore lips threatening speech
                        the Titan's loose robe
without Kent or Cordelia
              the eyelid's sewn purse
                        holding something back
or shut against too much light

FADING CHAMELEONS

No longer invisible,
you can tell us
from other lizards
by old habits of our vocation.

Abandoned wizardry
and too-long lingering eyes,
chafed articulation,
worn, inappropriate clothes.

MRS. WU

In '57, he went to see the new Russian.
The great helmsman said, *Rap the guy's knuckles.*
That's no way to behave when Joe ain't hardly dead.
Destalinize ... Destabilize!
And Enlai said to Kruschev,
You've taken too much land.

The fat peasant called him bourgeois.
Zhou was still smiling.
Who says we've nothing in common?
We've each betrayed our class.
And he told the story and heard it told again
in Warsaw, Budapest, Belgrade ...

Two years before in Bandung:
We must not forget, as Asians,
the first atom bomb fell on our continent ...

You know those stories. Long before,
my husband called him blood brother
and paid for his study in Kyoto.

He knew too little Japanese
and, with nothing to spend, took
the woman's part,
clearing the futon and sweeping the room.

In the evenings, we ate what he cooked.
He clung to the wine bottle and argued with Wu.
A strong leader is worthless, unless the people learn.
'And what is strong drink worth?', I asked.
Zhou looked for a broom and next day brought me flowers.

There was blossom for nine days in Maruyama park.
Now nowhere in Kyoto is that bittersweet scent.
Many died. Too many with his name on.
And he too died early, before Zedong,
the word *poems* ambiguous on his lips.

TIDYING UP

Yesterday, an hour of daylight left,
we cut our losses, knowing not much would be achieved.
You settled an old bill. I dug a hole
ready to replant the Christmas tree. Then together
we lifted the wet fencing that had fallen on the lawn
and humped it down the garden to lean against
the shed. I looked back at the pale latticed square
the fence had left, straw-coloured, circled by flies.
I watched you walk back in the house and turn
to see me watching still. I wedged the sodden
wood behind a line of bricks, careful
of the dank and naked hawthorn to one side.

Upstairs, once it was already dark,
you found your brooch was missing from your blouse.
You almost mourned the tapestry cameo and its metal
Victorian frame, fallen somewhere to grass. This morning,
feeling how much less of loss I know than you,
I poked in the black mulch around the evergreen
and scanned the struggling grasses without luck.
Carelessly, I emptied the old dustbin filled with rain
of a McEwan's can, a Mickey Mouse shoebag, and
– in a shock of grey and white – this still fresh squirrel
that must have slipped and drowned.

So I had to dig another hole
in a patch where nothing much would grow,
remembering as I edged the pale belly on the spade
a scampering through autumn to the pile of nuts,
acorns mostly, the children had gathered nearby.
Other squirrels may come to the garden;
that tree may well take root. I hope

we find your brooch or another like it;
but however carefully we watch each other,
your mother and your father won't come back.

PORNOGRAPHY

The day was ending. Darkening air
>would soon take home from labour each
>animal that walks the earth. On this field too

feet stamped. Misty skeins of breath
>rose from lips that glistened like Mackay's
>whose tongue lolled now over his lower teeth

as he eyed the ball for the place-kick.
>His team mates were taller and more fair
>than Donnelan's broad-shouldered, brown-stubbled

brutes. Consider, for example, their
>saggy-buttocked lock as the scrum breaks.
>Consider the flapping breeze-blown folds of fat

on pumping stumpy legs as he retreats.
>Consider this; and then compare the pale
>blue-veined marble of our three-quarter's firm

muscled upper thigh, glimpsed when he
>feeds the ball back from a further maul.
>Note the stud-marks bloody there, for neither team

is entirely naked. Note the hooker's
>commitment to the game, how, breaking away,
>he cuts down space, runs, swerves and keeps possession.

Note his mastery of grubber, chip and punt.
>Rewind the tape. For this is more than just
>another of O'Driscoll's stories. Try to ignore

the penny-sized needle bruises in close-up.
>None of our men are users. Scorn our opponents'
>chilled pillocks. Celebrate flesh returned to its element

of earth, the insistent inscription of rain.

ECHOES

They called it the second summer of love
but they dressed as if for the first.
Clive's sawdust-red hair hung lank
and long as Zal Yanovsky's and
Indira peered at the Browning essay
that poked out of her copy of Vogue
through Janis Joplin's specs.

Even their teacher, pushing forty,
could risk a narrow paisley-patterned tie.
A late September sun blessed
the afternoon and their lesson took alight.
Passion outraced wit as the first act closed;
the hall and imagined hills rang
to Olivia's, Viola's reverberate love.

The one he shared a name with had
the wild hair and quizzing eyes of Tim
Buckley on the cover of *happy sad* .
He had so much to say at first; then started
coming late, missed lessons, disappeared
for weeks, returned and half explained.
Promises were made. He vanished once again.

He sent a postcard from New York:
dog-sitting in a loft. Then home
and hospital. Was it the drugs they said
he sold that fried his brain? The gossiping
air knew best. He came for a reference
with his Macedonian girlfriend;
each of them a gentle refugee.

CUSTOMS OF THE PROVINCE

The legends concerning
how we appear on the surface
of a lake or a much slid-on stone
are a requirement of faith.

In the pale early years,
a white costume was called for.
Now we mostly sleep and eat.

A forklift-truckful of bamboo
passes through the best of us
between darknesses.

In memory of the girl
whose skin was peach-blossom
we dip our hands and feet in pitch.

In memory of the tiger's anger
and our sad survival here,
we wipe our eyes with stained hands.

So you stare at us
and we return your gaze,
looking out sparingly
from behind twin moons of kohl.

YES IT IS

It was something to do with the two of us
learning to drive so late; and that collection
of misplaced singles, B-sides, E.P. tracks

and oddities like 'Komm, Gib Mir Deine Hand'
came with us on our first car trip across country.
The A40. Dennis Potter's road. From Metroland

past Oxford, stopping at Birdlip to glimpse half-
remembered hills, picnicking in the Forest of Dean,
then down through valley-heads to my parents' home.

There were moments of terror: an articulated
lorry pulling into our lane just as we passed
its tail-gate; and anxieties about direction,

and moments of dreadful fatigue. The boys
counted legs of pub signs. And the tape helped:
the early songs most. Ringo's 'Matchbox'

holding his nose, *jealous* rhyming with *as well as*
over a repeated rhythmic chord, and then
that song nobody quite recalled, as if it had been

lying in wait for our early middle age.
Three-part harmony. John and George
obliterating Paul, Liverpool masking Detroit.

Red and *blue* and the unspoken *black*,
as Lennon's voice splintered in the bridge,
mourning his mother as you mourned yours.

AFTER NERUDA

Sometimes he's tired of being a man.
The reflection he sees, in shopwindows
or the cinema screen, takes on a sad
substance, tired and withered: ash-stains
on a shiny piece of suit cloth.

The gents hairdressers, with its cocktail
of smells, stings him to tears.
He wants the sleep of wool or old stones,
to see nothing of enterprises or gardens,
nothing of merchandise, spectacles, lifts.

He's tired of his feet, of toe-clippings,
of hair everywhere. Of his shadow.
He's just tired of being a man,
waking like a root in a dark cellar,
absorbing, thinking, counting the dead.

And Monday is the screech of a tyre,
or a sudden petrol flare.
It sees him coming with his prison face,
sends him to hospitals where bones fall out of
the windows, to damp and vinegary stores.

So he walks around, for peace, for forgetfulness,
past caged birds the colour of sulphur, tripe,
dentures in a coffee pot, surgical appliances,
and old men's underclothes hanging from a line,
dripping their slow, dirty tears.

A SALESMAN IN THE LAKES

West. Waste. Wastwater with its shifting scree
stirs in Stanley's inner eye, as he stops for petrol
south of Cleator Moor, noting the No to Nirex signs,
but thinking of the play: *Inside His Head.*

The abandoned title sends him back to the primal scene,
the bare boards in the blue box by Derwentwater,
the simple table where son and father fight.
Stanley remembers where he first heard these words.

Too big to fit on the 405 lines of the family screen,
the monstrous father raged. Stanley applauded
the younger Loman's cry. *You fake. You phoney little fake.*
Now Stanley knows too well the heaviness

that lumbers from small deception to unmeant mistake.
Arriving at last, he checks publicity, bookings,
trying to forget the image of a man he now resembles
slumped in a lay-by, asleep he hopes, at the wheel.

TACT

Unannounced, you sidled
rather than stumbled
into this dream of a blazing
family row. Sitting it out
modestly, looking not unembarrassed
at my performance, moving
your clenched broad fingers
between one another, flexing them
in a gesture between exasperation
and prayer.
                    My hectoring voice
wavers as you look abashed at me,
like that skateboarder halting suddenly,
as the hearse climbed the hill to your last
view of the lighthouse and the pier.

You didn't speak, but sat,
an unobtrusive visitor.
Your wild white hair, your moustache
like crests of foam, looking
not neatly combed and stiff
as we saw them in the chapel of rest,
but as I saw you last alive,
guiding my fledgling driver's eye
to the parking space by the hospital doors.

Or more than twenty years before,
after the last great flare of adolescence,
waking early and without rancour
to drive me to the station and my friends.
Or earlier still, on the day of my sister's birth,
calming us into the car with words

of the love sons owe to mothers and warnings
against taking sides.
                              Which quieten
my raised voice now, accustom me
to a long and patient view
over the perturbed and placid-seeming bay
where, without you, I must learn
your watchful, unassertive gift.

CELLULAR

We'd grit our teeth in trains as the brash
human resources manager turned the seat
next to us into her office, or blush
as privacies invaded
our poorly air-conditioned space.

But we had also seen a strong jaw soften,
a head tilting towards its own shoulder,
murmuring to the small world
it cradles and creates. And smiled
as the straight-faced colleague
danced in the car park,
her head back, laughing
like someone living on another plane.

And we would later hear how,
in Manhattan, a husband tapped again
the digits he had tried to reach all day
beneath rubble, atoms, ashes, dust
until the voice mail's memory could take
no more spoken words or text.

CHEZ HAYNES

Leroy Haynes, an Alabaman on a GI tour,
enjoyed these open streets where you could
face a white man eye to eye and not say 'sir'
or tip your head. Football player, actor,
sociologue and cook – Haynes turned a new
tongue to the lilt of the South and organised.

He set up his soulfood kitchen in Montmartre.
The photos on the wall of the jazz greats
and fifties movie stars trumpet his success;
Baldwin, Chester Himes and Richard Wright
argued the protest novel in Haynes Grill.
Tonight the singer and guitarist play 'Yesterdays'

In back, his Portuguese widow, Maria,
prepares pan-fried sausages, or ham hocks
and gabbage with cornbread on the side.
She lets the DC girl wait tables, looking in
shyly now and then to see what small
differences a life makes in the crowded world.

THE LENGTH OF SPRING

Peace is possible. The Amnesty dove's
still stickered to the window of the house
we didn't buy from you. And now you're housed
in a wicker coffin, a hamper of
the good things you were and will be, in the love
of your still friends, in the Friends' meeting house.
We stay to watch your children shoulder the spades
they dug into the moist earth to cover you;
and talk as if words could recover you
to the cold air, to the light's sharpest blades.

The same fierce brightness picks out the parade
against the war, and we remember you
at the month's end as we move shoe and shoe
ahead along the Embankment, early
arrivals buying new badges, nearly
losing one another by Westminster tube
and dawdling down Whitehall, enjoying the true
absurdity of *Make Tea Not War*. Dearly
the young in black entwine themselves for warm,
lest love fail, should nothing stop the war.

Another world is possible. As the war
draws near, a slogan on a lapel draws
smiles and nods, but subdued by will and force
we stumble in. I cut out the war,
listening to Jacobi's *Iliad* not the news,
until the statues start to fall across
the screens and grudging praise of 'moderate loss'
rises around us like the dusty haze
from crazed cuneiform tablets – to confuse
what's left of the clear light we would trust.